Shamanic
HEALING

Oracle Cards

Michelle A. Motuzas

4880 Lower Valley Road • Atglen, PA 19310

Designed by John P. Cheek
Type set in Mason Serif/Minion Pro

ISBN: 978-0-7643-5036-8
Printed in China
11 10 9 8

Published by Schiffer Publishing, Ltd.
4880 Lower Valley Road
Atglen, PA 19310
Phone: (610) 593-1777; Fax: (610) 593-2002
E-mail: Info@schifferbooks.com

For our complete selection of fine books on this and related subjects, please visit our website at www.schifferbooks.com. You may
also write for a free catalog.

This book may be purchased from the publisher. Please try your
bookstore first.

We are always looking for people to write books on new and
related subjects. If you have an idea for a book, please contact us at
proposals@schifferbooks.com.

Dedication

To my boys, Alex and Ian, who help
everything make sense to me. To my
parents, who gave me a solid foundation of love and truth. To Kathryn,
who has suspended disbelief on many
occasions just to support me.
To Bety Comerford and Steve Wilson,
for lighting my way. Finally, to the
peeps at the Yurt who always asked
for more and more art.

TRUST YOURSELF.
YOU KNOW MORE THAN
YOU THINK YOU DO.

—BENJAMIN·SPOCK

Contents

PREFACE

There are many different interpretations of Shamanism. Most indigenous cultures over the centuries have had members of their tribe or village who were considered Shamans—those men and women the people went to when they were sick or troubled. In retrospect, we sometimes look at them as "witch doctors" or as misguided people who relied on superstitious folklore without any scientific proof. We have now come back to revering the old ways: reading signs and tapping into the energy of an issue to assist with dealing more efficiently with our day-to-day struggles and challenges.

In regards to this deck of oracle cards, Shamanism is regarded as "endeavoring to connect with the energy of all living things." To do this, we must first recognize that everything is energy. Every thought, action, person, animal, and place is energy.

They hold different vibrations, but it is still all energy.

Energy vibrates at different speeds or vibrations. The vibrations of an energy can be the difference between being a dog or a chair! We hear a lot about the Law of Attraction. Like attracting like. Energy attracts equal energy.

Different energy patterns exist in our lives. Remember back to a time when you were sad—how "heavy" did your energy feel? How about the first stages of being in love? How light and buoyant did you feel?

As someone who has studied Shamanism and the workings of energy, I try to keep my vibrations high. I know this assists me in attracting the best possible path and the highest lessons to myself. Does this mean I won't suffer, get angry, or have "bad" things happen to me? No.

As humans walking on this earth, we need challenges to grow and learn. My wish is for you is to be able to face your challenges with wisdom, courage, and faith. Know that by bringing these attributes into your daily life, your challenges can be met with grace and ease.

The symbols and images used in this deck have originated through many of my own personal life experiences, but also borrow from universal symbols harking back to early man and cave drawings. I spent quite a few years in the Pacific Northwest. While there, I became enamored with the art of the native tribes. The graphic nature and strong symbolism really spoke to me.

As a humanities major in college, most of my classes were either art history or ancient cultures. I became fascinated with symbols in pre- and early Christian art. I always tell clients who come to me for a reading/drawing that symbols have certain meanings to me, but if one has a more intimate and personal one for you, that trumps mine! As an example: when I started doing these drawings, I would practice by holding one of my fellow Shaman students in my thoughts and draw whatever came to me. At the next class I would lay them out on the floor and, inevitably, the person I

11

held in my thoughts was drawn to the card I drew with them in mind. One woman picked "her" drawing and asked me about the symbols. One was a pomegranate, which I typically do not get very often. To me it means a rebirth or spring-like awakening (due to the Greek/Roman myth of Persephone), but the symbols were not coming together in a coherent manner. Something was out of place. This drawing was mostly about family messages from the other side. My friend happened to mention, "Oh, pomegranates always reminds me of my dad, he was from Iran and gave me a little pomegranate-shaped box from there. I miss him." Bingo! The pomegranate was a sign from her dad! I have since learned not to think too hard about what I get. It will all come together in the end!

Whether you are using these oracle cards for yourself, or reading for someone else, it is my hope that they will give you another tool for your toolbox and enable you to face whatever your life path has brought your way.

How to Do a Reading for Yourself and Others

———⬦⬦⬦———

There is no right or wrong way to do an oracle card reading for you or another person. It is a very personal and instinctual process. However, if you are new to this process, here are a few steps to get you started

First, become familiar with your cards. Hold them, look at them, feel them. Become one with them. How do they feel to you? Comforting? Energized? Uneasy? Connect with them.

———⬦⬦⬦———

Ground

Now I want you to ground your energy, or connect to the earth. If you have a favorite way of grounding, do this now. If you are new to the concept of grounding your energy into the earth, here is a great way to practice. Visualize two red balls about two feet below the soles of your feet. In your mind's eye, see beams of pure, white light from Creator coming in through the crown or top of your head.

Visualize and feel this light come down through your crown, past your throat, down into your heart region. Next, feel it travel through your solar plexus, belly, hips, down past your knees, and out the bottoms of your feet to connect with the red balls. Now reverse this visualization. Feel the white light from the red balls travel up through the soles of your feet, past your knees, hips, belly, again to your heart, throat, and out the top of your head. You should feel the bottoms of your feet tingling. This not only helps prepare you to do a reading, but this technique can be used throughout your day whenever you feel a need to "ground out" stuck emotions or feelings. The amazing aspect of this exercise is that after a while of consciously practicing this visualization, you will feel your body automatically do it when you need to ground.

Shuffle

When you are ready to start the reading, shuffle the cards. If you are doing this reading for yourself, think of the subject matter you want a reading on. If you have a specific question, concentrate on that. If you are doing this for someone else, have them shuffle the cards. You will know when to stop the shuffle. The person who is shuffling may hear an inner voice say "Now" or "Stop" or "Here." Or they may just have a "Knowing."

Lay Out the Cards

Lay out your cards in the layout you have

decided on. (The following section will have some sample layouts and ideas on creating your own.)

* * *

Scan

Take some time to scan the cards that have been chosen. Notice any repeating symbols. This will indicate an overall theme for the reading. For example, raindrops are a common theme in many of the cards. Raindrops = water = emotions. This can be a sign of overwhelming emotions playing a part in the question asked. While the symbols for each card differ, you need to also take the whole of the cards that are drawn together.

This is also a time when you want to empty your mind of any preconceived ideas on what the cards "should" say. Let the images enter your subconscious. Let them speak to you. If any of the symbols I have used have a specific, different meaning than what is written in this book, let that enter into the reading. This is part of the intuitive process.

READ THE CARDS

Start with the first card in the layout and find the definition in this book. The cards are designed to be read both on their own and in conjunction with the cards surrounding them. This may seem daunting at first, but as you become familiar with the cards, their meanings and the different layouts, this will become more and more effortless to you. If you have ever driven a car with manual transmission, it is a lot like that! Remember when you had to really think and say to yourself "Clutch, shift, clutch, gas"? After a while, you didn't have to think about that anymore; it became automatic!

This isn't a one-size-fits-all process. These cards are meant to facilitate a conversation—either with yourself and your guides or the person you are reading for. They will assist you in seeing the truth to the energy surrounding the situation that is being inquired about.

―――――∞◎◎―――――

SUMMARIZE

At the end of the reading, after going through the cards in the layout, you can summarize for yourself or the person you are reading for.

ORACLE CARD LAYOUTS

———⟨◦⟩———

There are numerous different layouts you can use for an oracle card reading. They can be as simple or as complex as you like. Many of the traditional Tarot card layouts, such as the Celtic Cross, the Mandela Spread, and the Tree of Life Spread work amazingly well with oracle cards. Here are some that I personally use, going from simple to complex.

———⟨◦⟩———

THE SINGLE-CARD LAYOUT

This is an easy and fast reading that can actually be pretty complex. It will make you think deeply about a question that you perhaps thought was a little above needing a yes or no answer.

Simply shuffle the cards as directed and choose the first card on the top of the deck. Sometimes I add to the complexity by looking at the last card to determine the foundation of the question being asked (this can be done for all of the layouts).

EXAMPLE:

Mary wants to know: "Is my new job going to be long term?"

The **Inner Journey** card was selected.

This card is all about respecting the journey of a soul and not focusing on the outcome. With some discussion, Mary realized she had been going from job to job looking for that "perfect" fit. In hindsight, she never gave any of her positions a chance to bring her where they were meant to. She would jump ship at a particular job if it did not fit into her view of how her life should be going.

When I looked at the card at the bottom of the deck, it was **Struggle**. This indicated that the energy surrounding the issue of Mary and her perfect job quest was a life lesson for her. She needed to just sit tight and let her road unfold how it is supposed to, without labeling it or placing a judgment on where she was compared to where she thought she should be.

A year later, through her seemingly imperfect job, Mary was promoted to the job of her dreams. This never would have happened if she had kept on moving between positions!

The Three-Card Layout

This is another simple and fast layout. Traditionally, the cards are shuffled and placed from left to right. The far left card indicates the past, the middle card the present, and the card on the right represents the future.

You can actually assign any meaning to each card placement that you want.

EXAMPLE:
Becky had a question: "What do I do about John?"

I want the first card drawn to represent how this situation with John came about (Past). **Abundance** was drawn.

The second card will represent the energy surrounding the situation right now (Present). **Trust** was drawn.

The third will offer a path to take to help this situation become resolved (Future). **A New Day** was drawn.

Again with this spread, I will most likely look at the card at the bottom of the deck to get an inkling of the foundation of this issue, **Death**.

After going over and discussing the cards with Becky, it was clear that when she had entered into a relationship with John, abundance was everywhere. Lots of time spent together, evenings out. Like most new loves, everything was wonderful! (Abundance)

By now, however, the relationship has cooled down a bit. John is no longer trying to impress Becky as much as he had when they first got together. Becky thinks that it has to do with John losing interest in her and their relationship. The card drawn for the present (Trust) urges her to not make any rash decisions or assumptions about John's feelings.

The foundation card (Death) indicates to her that a change is coming, and the possible outcome card (A New Day) indicates that if she trusts the flow of the relationship, she would turn a corner in it.

The outcome for Becky was more than she had hoped for. Both she and John realized through this transformation in their relationship that they had to focus their energy, not on one another, but on a third party...the relationship itself!

The Five-Card Layout

A five-card spread will give you a little more depth in the answers it offers. As the spreads above, shuffle the cards and lay them out in a line from left to right.

Card 1: Represents the relevant past.
Card 2: Represents the energy surrounding the situation right now.
Card 3: Indicates possible hidden issues affecting the situation.
Card 4: Indicates a possible action to take for the highest possible outcome.
Card 5: Represents the most likely outcome.

Steve wants to know: "Will I be moving in the next six months?"

The cards pulled:
Card 1: **Retreat**
Card 2: **Planting Seeds**
Card 3: **Self Love**
Card 4: **Male Energy**
Card 5: **Unlimited Possibilities**
Foundation card: **Emotional Release and Healing**

When looked at as a whole, the Sun, a symbol of action and male energy figures in three of the five cards drawn. This indicates that if Steve does want to move, it is going to come through ACTION on his part. This is not a situation that is going to just happen or resolve itself.

The card representing the past is **Retreat**, indicates that Steve has been hunkering down in the recent past, gathering his strength. The energy surrounding the situation is **Planting Seeds**. If a move is something that Steve wants to occur, he needs to look around at his life to see where he can start planting the seeds for a move. He indicated that he has been thinking of saving some money for a future down payment. He also wants to clean up his credit score so he can be more competitive in the housing market. The **Self Love** card as the hidden issues was interesting. After some discussion, Steve realized that he was constantly having an ongoing dialogue in his head about his capability to purchase a new house. Due to a divorce and a layoff in his past, he had come to the conclusion that he wasn't capable of getting what he wanted in life. Most people who harbor this belief in their energy field are not aware of it. No one walks around saying that they are not capable or worthy. But with some digging, this false belief that they have carried with them comes to light and they can see the roadblocks the belief alone has put in their own path. The fifth card, Male Energy, gives the advice that, going forward, make things happen—face your fear of failure.

The Foundation card, Emotional Release and Healing summed up perfectly what on the surface looked to be a simple question of "Will I or won't I move in the next six months?" This was about Steve's journey towards healing, the moving issue was an outward symptom of a deeper wound that needed to be healed.

Steve continued to be aware of his inner dialogue, and worked on getting all his ducks in a row to be able to purchase his first house. With his proactive action, the Universe lined up for him and the perfect property was presented just at the right time, showing Unlimited Possibilities!

Notes on Interpretations

There are a few things I would like to note about reading with the *Shamanic Healing Oracle* deck. Unlike Tarot cards, there are no reversal meanings. These cards are a bit more straight forward.

> THE CLEARER YOU ARE WITH YOUR QUESTION, THE CLEARER THE CARDS WILL BE.

If, while shuffling, a card seems to "jump" out of the deck, take it and put it to the side. This is an indication that the energy in the card has a place in the reading, but more of a general place in the overall theme, rather than a specific meaning.

If nothing seems to resonate with the person being read for, entertain the idea that perhaps this reading is for the reader, or a person who has accompanied the person getting the reading. Many times, we are given what we *need* to know, not necessarily what we *want* to know.

Remember that at the end of the day, we all have free choice. What you see in a reading depends on the choices of all involved. It's a snapshot of the moment—an energetic snapshot, but one that can change course depending on the energy involved, a change or healing, and the choices made by the individuals involved.

ORACLE CARD
MEANINGS

I Movement into Balance

The sun balances the moon just as the earth, the water, and the sky remain in precious balance—so you are moving from unbalanced ideas and lifestyles into a more balanced way of being.

A situation may call for some tweaking to adjust it into a balanced mode. Look at the energy and emotions you are putting out into the universe, your world, your relationships, or goals. Balance that with the energy you are allowing yourself to receive. The body inherently tries to maintain a state of balance; so do our souls. If you are not receiving enough, you may be unconsciously giving more to restore a perceived "balanced" state. Step out of that automatic response and listen to your guides and your soul for what this situation truly warrants.

I Movement into Balance

2 New Beginnings

Water, emotion, energy, all life affirming and life giving. Patience is the key.

Once the deluge of emotion passes, you will see that left in its wake is a wondrous new day, a rainbow of possibilities. Do not get attached to the emotions that surround this situation. This will only attach your identification with the emotion itself—giving it more power and hindering the release, so that the door to your new beginning will not open. Sit in the emotion, cry, journal, talk it out with a friend, and then let it go. Perform a ritual if you are called to one. Place your feelings on a bit of paper and let it go—whether through water or fire (both excellent transmuting elements). Be thankful for the experience of the situation and proclaim to Creator that you are ready for the newness that is about to come into your life.

2 NEW BEGINNINGS

3 SLOW BUT STEADY

Don't rush the situation. More often than not divine timing and our timing are not the same!

When you try to speed up a life experience, a relationship or even a project, you circumvent necessary experiences or lessons along the way that will contribute to a perfect outcome. Know that wherever you are in this situation, it's the perfect place for you to be. If this place is causing you anxiety—perfect. Now you can look within and ask yourself why. What are your fears surrounding this perceived delay in getting to where you want to go? What is the worst that can happen? What is the best that can happen? What if we removed the words "best" and "worst" and just let things unfold at their own pace without attaching judgment?

3 SLOW BUT STEADY

4 Integrating Past, Present & Future

We all arrive on this earth with a plan. We all have lessons to learn. In the process of learning these lessons, most of us will encounter experiences that we will label as "bad." This labeling and duality we carry with us wherever we go is what we call our so-called "baggage." When we let these labels direct our reactions to life and experiences in the present, or even project them into the future, we are working with a lower-energy vibration.

When you are able to integrate your lessons without labels, then you are free to remain in the present experience and enjoy it for what it truly is. You can then move forward into the future without expectations or agendas and be much more open to what will be for our highest and best. Let go of labels and judgments surrounding this situation.

4 Past, Present & Future

5 Psychic Development

The energy and healing work you are doing now will enable you to heighten your sensitivity to the energy around you and others. This will assist you in developing discernment. Discernment is the feeling you get in your body that signals to you whether something feels right or wrong: your sixth sense, your gut feeling.

The situation you are inquiring about is asking you to use your discernment; you do not want to take on others' energy, yet you do not want to close yourself off out of fear. Envision energy—flowing through you like water. Take on too much and you can sink. Closing yourself off offers a very different energetic experience. When you let the water energy flow as it will, and neither embrace it or fight it, you are truly in the flow. Remaining at this elevated energetic vibration will allow you to tap into the realms of the psyche.

5 Psychic Development

Alternately, this card can signify a pull to take classes, workshops, or read books about psychic development.

6 Discernment

As spiritual, physical, and energetic beings, we oftentimes blur the lines between our energy, the energy of a situation, and the energy of another person. When we take on other people's energy and label it as our own, we start to judge. This lowers our energetic vibrations. We then get caught up in a seemingly never-ending cycle of feeling "bad," labeling, justifying, and appropriating what is not ours to claim.

The lesson here, as in the previous card, is to be present, not label or judge, and let the energy/feeling wash through you. Once you do this, notice where in your body you feel the effects of the emotion. Does your heart open up? Does your belly hurt? Does your throat get tight? Your head can lie to you, but your body never does. It is easy to become overwhelmed. Make a habit of making your first response to overwhelming energy: "Wow, that's interesting!" instead of "What's wrong with me?"

6 DISCERNMENT

This allows you to objectively discover how
and why your body is reacting to the given
situation or person. This card is asking you to
stop looking outside yourself for answers to
an issue. Instead, sit with it and listen to what
your body is telling you.

7 Reunion of Souls

There is a school of thought that says before our souls come to earth, we make contracts, or agreements, with other souls. At one point in time, we appear in each other's lives to assist those involved in learning a lesson, being a catalyst for a needed change, or to share in profound joy.

When a person comes into your life to teach you a lesson—no matter the human form, no matter the human experience—this agreement is based in love. The human experience may have been painful and extremely challenging—acknowledge the depth of love needed for this contract to take place and then let them go. The experience may have been profoundly moving, but ended abruptly and without reason. Again—be grateful and move on—cherish the lessons and move forward into your life the way it was meant to be.

7 Reunion of Souls

Alternately, this card signifies a profound "soulmate" relationship, whether it be between lovers, friends, or parents and children. Cherish the gift given.

8 Death

Death is scary. Endings—whether they are planned or a surprise—are most often accompanied with a sense of anxiety, unease, or more strongly with denial and refusal to let go of the person, relationship, or situation that is ending.

Endings always signify beginnings. As in the new beginning card, this card urges you to let go gracefully. Do not attach yourself to the emotions and the energy of what is ending. Feel it, experience it, and then let it go. A slight shift in perspective is sometimes all that is needed to experience this transition with grace and ease. Instead of thinking "oh no—I have to start all over!" shift your perspective slightly and think "Yay! I get to start all over!" This shift will raise your energetic vibrations and carry you through this time of change.

This card can also signify the ending of a troublesome situation.

8 Death

9 PERCEPTION

With energy, sometimes a slight shift in perception is all that's needed. Remember— nature strives to retain balance. It is only our perception and labels that cause us to think otherwise.

Is there a situation in your life that you are viewing from a very rigid perspective? Are you certain that you are at the center of all the drama around you? Perhaps cultivating the ability to step outside of the drama and see the issue from every different view point will shift your judgment of this person or situation from intolerable to simply "it is," and as it is, it won't remain so for long. Letting go of the tether that holds you to a certain viewpoint also frees the situation up to go the natural way and get back into balance.

9 Perception

10 Burden

Many times we take on the stress of those we love and care for. We see it as the ultimate sacrifice. We take on others' burdens to save them the trouble or heartache. Ironically, the way energy and the universe work makes this a very counterproductive way of operating. When we take on the burdens of others, we deny them the ability to learn and grow from their own lessons. We also interfere with divine planning and timing. Never one to be thwarted, any lessons circumvented will absolutely re-appear—sometimes with much more force than what was originally intended.

Ask yourself if you or another is taking on troubles and lessons not belonging to them out of a need to be needed. This stems from the fear that you (or they) are fundamentally not enough. This is not true. You are created perfect. Your fears and doubts keep you separated from this truth. This is the separation

10 BURDEN

one can feel from Creator. Once you accept and believe you are perfect and worthy, the tendency to make yourself invaluable to others through your help and assistance will go away. Your relationships can then be based on truth and not manipulation.

II New Day

A new day enables us to see in a brand new light. We can see more clearly once the shadows of fear and doubt are brushed away by the light of creation.

Once the initial shock of discovering the duality in a situation has worn off, you can find comfort that there truly is no bad or good. It just *is*. When this is realized, the possibilities for the outcome of a situation become endless.

This card also advises to wait. Everything regarding this situation has yet to unfold.

II New Day

12 TRUTH

The eagle proudly surveys its domain from such a high perch that all pertaining to this situation is revealed. The shadows hide nothing from his keen vision.

Once you can remove yourself from the muck that lower vibrations keep you in, you can attain a viewpoint that enables you to see the truth of the matter. This card advises you to search for the truth of the situation, regardless of the emotions it brings up. Are you or someone connected to you unconsciously suppressing the truth? Hiding from the truth can only intensify the lesson later on.

12 Truth

13 Abundance

Abundance takes on many forms: material possessions, friendships, excellent health, emotional stability, unique experiences…

When you lock yourself into a narrow view on what defines abundance, you lose out on the whole picture of what it could mean. Open yourself up to as many forms of wealth and abundance that are possible and watch your blessings multiply. Always remember that focusing on what you do not have is a sure-fire way to feed the energy and make that your truth. Every day watch for signs of abundance from the universe—acknowledge and be thankful, thus encouraging the continued flow of energy. Remember the universe will always provide you with what you need.

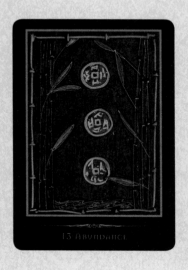

13 ABUNDANCE

14 Teaching

The situation you are inquiring about encourages teaching, whether it be student/teacher, parent/child or just friend/friend. We are, all of us, leaning and teaching constantly when we are maintaining a high vibration energetically.

Never despair that the seeds you have planted have failed to take root. They may be taking time to germinate, or they may have migrated to another field. Do not plant seeds with the expectation of an outcome. Disengage from the attachment to the outcome of the situation and move on. A farmer doesn't sit down next to the seeds he plants waiting for them to sprout. What a recipe for disappointment! He plants them and moves on. Never once does he second guess if he was doing the right thing in the right way. He simply does what he is called to do, and trusts that the fruits of his labor will be what they are supposed to be!

14. Teaching

This card also encourages a more formal teaching experience. Look for ways you can enrich others' lives through sharing your expertise and knowledge.

15 Honoring Your Energy

We all have those days when we are disinclined to do anything. We try all sorts of mental tricks to talk ourselves into doing what we "should" be doing. Does this ever work? No. We end up feeling guilty (a very low vibration) for not getting anything done, which causes us to try twice as hard the next day, which causes us to get overwhelmed and exhausted, which then leads to becoming caught up in a vicious cycle.

Your body has rhythms just as everything else on this earth does—flowers, trees, plants, and the elements. The tides ebb and flow, the sun and moon rise and set, animals hibernate, and flowers grow, bloom, and go dormant. You need to listen to the inherent cycles within you. Rest when you need to—work when you need to. Do not try to "outthink" the natural rhythms. Go easy on yourself and reserve judgment—you are your own harshest critic.

15 Honoring Your Energy

16 Masculine Energy

The sun—powerful, a life force without which nothing on this earth could survive. The masculine energy is one of action, doing, creating, forcing. In nature it is balanced out with feminine energy. When we find ourselves embodying this energy we get things done—we are thinking, logical beings. If we reside here too staunchly, we do not have any room for the opposite energy to come in. Being able to effortlessly flow from one to the other—masculine to feminine—is the pinnacle of being in the flow energetically. Sometimes in love relationships, the energy turns topsy-turvy and we end up residing in an energy that doesn't meet our highest need. This is hard to break out of due to fear: the fear of "If I don't do it, it won't get done."

Realize that two people make up a relationship and in an evolved one—the relationship itself develops its own energetic balance—a perfect combination of yin and yang—mas-

16 Masculine Energy

culine and feminine. If there is a void in one
area, an imbalance will develop and, as is the
nature of things, unconsciously we will try to
balance out. Being aware is a perfect first step.

Alternately, this card signifies a very
important man in your life.

17 Feminine Energy

Darkness. The moon. The tides. The quiet gestation before the chaos—the void. These are all aspects of feminine energy: passive, waiting, gestating, and nurturing. It is the opposite of the prior card: so very different, yet the perfect companion.

Perhaps you have yet to find your feminine side. The life you are leading right now has given you opportunities to embrace this part of you—but between the two opposing energies, feminine energy is the harder one to embrace. It requires trust and lack of fear. Trust that all is as it should be and the absence of the fear of "things" not getting done. Perhaps in the past you had been hurt when you were embracing your feminine energy—physically or mentally. This was the free will of the person who hurt you—it was not caused by being who you were. Do not let the actions of another dictate who

17 Feminine Energy

you need to be. Examine your feminine side—become friends with her again.

Alternately, this card represents an important woman in the seeker's life.

18 It's All Good

Every experience you have in your lifetime
has the potential to be a teaching tool. By
remembering and embracing this idea,
the situations you encounter become less
fraught with unneeded emotion and drama.
By not attaching labels or expectations to
people and situations, you allow the pure
divine energy to flow unimpeded.

While you may have little control over
what happens *to* you at times, you always
have control over how you react. Do you
react on an impulse? Strike out at others
when you feel hurt? Do you crawl into your
safe place when the world seems mean and
hurtful? Face this challenge in your life
head on. Be thankful for the opportunity to
experience whatever it is that is happening.
Set yourself a goal of learning from every
situation in your life. Find that silver lin-
ing. It's there.

18 It's All Good

19 Unlimited Possibilities

When fall turns into winter, the leaves fall from the trees, birds fly south, plants go dormant—some even die having lived the life they were meant to. Do we ever panic and wallow in the fear that this is it? There will never be another robin singing?! There will never be another ripe tomato? No we don't. Why is that? We know that after winter, spring will return, followed by the bounty of summer.

It is so in your life. At any given time, there are unlimited possibilities for you and yours, many different paths to take, many different options available. Do not get bogged down into thinking in a linear fashion. Open your eyes and your heart, and feel the power your free will and choice brings to you. Make your life what it is meant to be.

19 UNLIMITED POSSIBILITIES

20 HEALING ENERGY

Drawing this card guides you to work with energy on a healing level. Take a class, go and receive a Reiki healing, or just sit in meditation and concentrate on mindfulness. With the healing energy of Divine love, you do not have to "know" how to do anything. Just sit quietly, set your intention and let Creator's love fill you up.

When you are living in a vibration of healing, you not only affect yourself, but those around you. Others then can connect with your energy and their vibrations can rise as a result. There is no force to this. This is basically how energy works. Your vibrational charge will effect change in the ones you are close to.

Alternately this card signifies healing is taking place within a relationship.

20 HEALING ENERGY

21 SACRED SPACE

Find a spot in your home or office that you can access easily. Create a sacred spot just for you. This will be a place for you alone.

If space is at a premium, then a shelf or corner will do. Put here only those items that hold significant meaning to you and touch you on a deep, personal level. Examples are photos of loved ones, rocks, feathers, shells. Place a candle, even if it cannot be lit. This signifies the element of fire and represents the flame of Creator's love for you; the fire of creation, or purification. Perhaps fire means something entirely different to you. Use this space to go to daily—even if it's just for a few moments—to ground and calm yourself. Working this into your daily routine will bring you to a place of greater understanding.

21 SACRED SPACE

22 Transformation

After the rain comes the sun—after the caterpillar comes the butterfly. This situation you are inquiring about is somehow acting as a catalyst for a major transformation.

If you find yourself questioning or having regrets—don't. Try not to second guess yourself, or beat yourself up. Nothing happens that is not supposed to. Many of your issues and situations are not anything to be upset about. They are a path to wholeness. You are the one who infuses drama and chaos into the situation. You are always given opportunities to grow and learn. Growth and learning very rarely come about when everything stays status quo and just as you think they should. Be thankful you have this wonderful opportunity to transform and heal to a better and higher rate of vibration!

22 Transformation

23 Forgiveness

It has been said forgiveness is the greatest gift we can give ourselves—forgiveness of others, but also forgiveness of self. We are the most critical and judgmental of ourselves. This inner critic does so much more harm than criticism that comes from others.

Forgive yourself for trusting others and getting hurt, for not knowing, for not seeing, for not believing. You are human and you are growing and learning. Human perfection is rooted in imperfection. This card indicates the need for forgiveness in the situation asked about.

23 Forgiveness

24 Ascension

Some of those following a spiritual path have Ascension as the ultimate goal. However, Ascension, portrayed in art and literature as a great leap into instant nirvana, is actually a giant work of, well...art and fiction! Rather, Ascension is the process of conscious living. We are all spiritual beings. We are all souls in a human body who are living life on this earth in order to learn and to grow at the soul's level. That is being spiritual.

Whether you are conscious of it or not, you are walking towards ascension. Each experience, relationship, obstacle, joy and creation, will bring you one step closer on the ladder to where we all end—with a greater awareness of ourselves than we started out with. This situation, at its best, is a rung on the ladder of your soul's path towards ascension.

24 Ascension

The situation you are inquiring about is assisting you on this ladder. Work at the bigger picture and know you are bigger than any issues or problems you may have.

25 Sexual Energy

In the purest sense, sexual energy is not an energy to be expanded from you. It is a state to reside in. The first and second chakras are the root of our sexual feelings. When you use this very potent energy to manipulate people and situations, you are doing yourself a huge disservice. When you expand your life force energy up from your first two chakras and incorporate the energy from your heart and your crown, you can experience the most complete and Divine experience of sexual energy possible. This doesn't even have to include another person. When you can merge your connection to Creator with your connection to the earth, without any filters or blocks between the two, you will experience a complete and true connection.

We act as the conduit between heaven and earth. And when we can put ourselves

25 SEXUAL ENERGY

into this energy at any given time, we are not tempted to use our sexual energy in a way that feeds our need for validation. Nor are we easily manipulated by another's outputting of sexual energy. This card is asking you to look at where sexual energy is directed in your life.

26 Duality

Black and white/good and evil/yes and no/ up and down and want/don't want. These are all examples of dualistic thinking. What if you banned these labels from your thoughts for a day? What would happen? Would the world end? Doubtful. Would some person "get away" with something. No. Would you attach less emotion to a "bad" situation or drama. Possibly. If that happened and there was less attachment to a situation, you could keep your vibrations higher, which would enable you to deal more successfully with any situation that comes your way.

Given enough time—most "bad" situations work out in the end. It is your choice to be drama free, or spend a lot of time and energy wasted on a situation that will turn out okay in the end? What do you choose?

26 Duality

27 Stripping Illusions

The lotus flower is a funny plant. It flourishes in the muck and mud. Apparently, in spite of the muck of its birth, beautiful petals open up, layer after layer, revealing more and more of its inner beauty. You are being called to strip away illusion after illusion from your life! You are being asked to enable your true essence to shine through! Allow layer after layer of false beliefs, cluttered thinking, unfulfilling relationships, chaotic environments, to go by the wayside to reveal the perfect essence of your core self.

This process is challenging at best. We tend to hold on to the illusions we have created, thinking they keep us safe. All they really do is to blind us to our true beauty and potential. This card is calling to you to look your truth in the face and not let illusions cloud your view of the true beauty of yourself and others.

27 Stripping Illusions

28 ANGER

A very strong and primal emotion, anger sometimes catches us by surprise. At other times it seethes just under the surface, simmering a long while until it boils over, scalding anyone who is close.

Anger is based in fear. Fear of loss of control, fear of not being loved, fear of being judged, fear of not being enough. When anger enters your life—be it yours or someone else's—go beneath the surface and try to address the real fear that has triggered it. Anger doesn't go away without addressing the underlying fear.

Alternately, beware of someone's anger directed towards you.

28 Anger

29 Changes

Like ripples from the smallest drop of water in a pond, the smallest of changes in one's life can bring about the greatest rewards.

Think about changes you can make in your life. These do not have to be grand, sweeping changes. Judicious, small changes can add up to life changes after time. Think about small changes you can make now that will add to your quality of life: clean out clutter, commit to walking every night after dinner, cut out processed food from your life.

Alternately—big changes are coming your way.

29 Changes

30 Divine Timing

How often do you feel that you want things in your life to change NOW? Not two years from now, not even two months, but: Right. This. Instant! Seldom do we see the whole picture of why our lives are unfolding the way they are. We don't need to. What we need to do is surrender to the way things are right now. This doesn't mean to not take action when a situation in untenable. What it means is to let your life unfold before you so that you have access to all the information, all the lessons, and all the people you will need to go where you are headed.

Divine timing is at work in this situation. Try not to fight it. Instead go within during meditation and ask the questions you want answers to: "why not now?" "how can I best prepare myself?" "what lessons do I need to learn prior to the change I want to see?" You will get answers.

30 Divine Timing

31 Omens

Hawks are messengers. This majestic bird flies high and reaches the realms of the spirit. They bring back messages from both the seen and unseen.

Drawing this card speaks of focus and intuition. Pay attention to the coincidences in your life right now. Focus on where you want to go—how high do you want to fly? When you see a hawk, someone is trying to get your attention. Pay attention to serendipity in your life. Be glad, for this is a reminder that you are living in the flow of energy. Things will soon shift for you.

31 Omens

32 Struggle

Struggle is a part of this life—so much so that you probably know people who seem to constantly attract one struggle after another into their lives. This is their comfort zone. While struggle is natural, it is natural only so far as it lends itself to learning lessons and overcoming inner personal challenges. Beneath every one of these struggles is the gift of enlightenment. The satisfaction of a lesson learned. Use this knowledge as the light at the end of your dark tunnel. What lesson is this struggle teaching you?

Alternately, after a brief setback, this situation will start to right itself.

32 STRUGGLE

33 Integration

We are a sum of all our experiences in this and other lives. We all bring forward a wealth of knowledge, talents, and wisdom. One of the challenges is remembering who we are. We are bombarded every day in every way with messages on who we *should* be, what we *should* do, what we *should* wear, how we *should* live…. These messages coming from the media, society, our family and friends, and even strangers can drown out who we really are meant to be: who we have grown into lifetime after lifetime.

Find some quiet moments in your day to identify and start a relationship with that small, strong voice inside you. Pretty soon you won't hear the other messages. Many times in your interactions with others, you hear that small voice that tells you something is not right. Your logical mind tells you to stop it, nothing is wrong, stop being silly/dramatic/over reacting. You may ignore your inner voice

33 Integration

in a quest to fit in, to be loved or admired. You do not realize that your inner voice is warning you that the other person's energy is not matching their words or actions. Listen to your instincts about this situation or person.

34 Ancient Wisdom

Nature is the perfect place to center yourself and ground out any excessive noise in your head. In nature, all the secrets of the universe are held: from the fiercest energy of a raging sea in a storm to the nurturing and loving energy of a hundred year old grove of trees. Get out in nature and listen to what she has to tell you. There is much to learn from nature. Trees just want to be trees. They are not trying to be boulders. Deer are just deer; they accept that. Wolves are wolves. They know no other way; they do not try to get an extreme makeover to become a bear.

This energy vibration can be so different than the human experience. It is pure love, non-judgment, and acceptance. When you tap into the ancient wisdom of the natural world, you find peace within yourselves. You get to "know thyself." By drawing this card, you are being asked to come to peace with who you are and what you have to offer the situation.

34 Ancient Wisdom

35 Inner Journey

Not all who wander are lost. At times we are so consumed with our own personal journey that we project our journey onto another. Every soul arrives on this planet with lessons to learn and a life to live. For as many souls that are out there, there are that many different journeys.

Do not judge another's journey—always respect where another person is on their path. Meet everyone you come in contact with where they are on their path. Do not insist they come to where you are. By doing this, you will not only expose those around you to your own healing vibration, but you will offer them acceptance without judgment. This is a great gift to both give and receive.

35 Inner Journey

36 GROUNDING

As humans, our bodies are of the earth. It is a natural inclination when we experience uncomfortable emotions or energy to "ground it out," much in the way a ground wire works with electrical current. However, with so much in our modern lives that causes us to be disconnected from Creator, we tend to gravitate towards "false grounding." Overeating, smoking, drinking, and recreational drugs are common ways some try to ground. These items are *of* the earth—but they are not *the* earth. This is not a true grounding—and as such it cannot sustain. It doesn't last. What ends up happening is that, as with most experiences that are false, we need more and more to achieve the same result.

To truly ground and connect to both the earth and Creator, practice consciously connecting your energy to the earth. You should not be getting your energy outside yourself, but directly from the Divine. This is achieved

36 GROUNDING

through meditation, energy work, and mindfulness. Find a way that works for you and practice it! By drawing this card, you are being asked to look at areas in your life where you may be employing false grounding as a coping mechanism.

37 Emotional Release

We all want to be strong. As humans we value strength and independence. But also as humans we need the support of our family, our friends, our tribe.

Trying so hard to be strong, pushing down emotions such as fear, anger, betrayal, sadness, only forces them to grow and become stronger. The bubbling up and release that eventually comes takes everyone involved by surprise, and sometimes does harm in terms of hurt feelings and words that cannot be taken back. Get into the practice of voicing your feelings—even if it's just acknowledging them to yourself. Journal, create, dance. Find a way that you can safely feel your most feared emotions. Feel them and then let them go. This is a potentially deep healing for you.

37 Emotional Release

38 Growth

This situation or time is one of rapid growth. The seeds that have been planted have germinated and taken root. Go with the flow of this growing time. You may find people and situations falling away from your life, as now they do not serve who and what you are becoming. It may be that your vibration no longer resonates with theirs. It's okay—wish them well, be grateful for what they brought to you and you to them, and send them on their way. Room has now been made for new experiences, people, and situations to help you to your next level.

If you are not feeling this shift right now, be prepared because it will soon come to pass.

38 GROWTH

39 Creativity

This is a profoundly creative time period for you—whether it is in the traditional arts, music, or writing—or it could be a new curiosity about exploring a way to funnel your creative urges. To be creative, you need to access your right brain—your emotional, sensing, feeling center. Do this by trying things you've never done before—get physical, dance, doodle.

When we acknowledge and act upon our impulse to create, we are aligning our will with the Creator. In this we can experience the flow of being on your highest path. Start creating and notice how time has no meaning anymore. Hours fly by before you realize it. It is not a struggle. It is pure inspiration.

This card can also signify a birth of a child, or of a whole new way of being!

39 Creativity

40 Retreat

This is a good time to retreat into your safe place, a quiet time to gather your resources for what's to come. Work on making your body, mind, and soul as strong and unencumbered as possible. This is the card that urges you to get your "ducks in a row" for the changes that lay ahead. Changes sometimes come fast and furious. Even when they are longed for, it can take us unprepared. By drawing this card, you are advised to prepare for some changes coming your way soon!

Alternately, take this time to process the changes that you have recently gone through.

40 Retreat

41 Self Love

We always try to think so highly of the ones we love. We even give strangers the benefit of the doubt. But when it comes to self-love, many of us fall woefully short. To love oneself is to accept imperfection, embrace learning and battle through the all-consuming fires of self-doubt in order to find the energetic balance inside each of us.

Be aware of the small, insidious voice that perhaps repeats the negative self-assessment you had as a child. Maybe an ex-lover or friend put a label on you that you've accepted. These self-judgments have no place in a whole, healthy relationship that is vital to have with yourself. It's only when you find your love for yourself that you can sincerely offer love to others.

41 Self Love

42 joy

We are created in joy. The balance of energy and higher vibrations brings us closer to divine love—pure joy. Joy can be a destination, but it can also be the vehicle that you use to get to that destination. Faith, grace, gratitude, and love all merge together, at different times and in different amounts, to create joy.

There is love, growth, tears, change, and self-realization in this card. This card portends a happy and joyous time.

42 | JOY

43 Letting Go

Letting go of a person or situation can be a challenge. At times, what's at stake is not just the relationship or situation, it's the attachment we had for it: the hopes, the dreams, the expectations. Many relationships end long past their natural ending point. One or both people hung on, hoping things would change. They invested so much time because without that person, or job, or relationship, their future loomed up as one big blank screen. For many this is too scary to bear. However, by letting go, we create a space for a person or situation that will resonate with us where we are now.

Start looking at your expectations. Try not to have any. This will enable you to live in the moment and be mindful in the present. To be able to gracefully release from a situation is a lesson for all of us.

43 Letting Go

44 Home

This card represents a homecoming of the soul, of finding your tribe, of coming home. The situation you are inquiring about has the potential to be a homecoming—a safe and secure place that both nourishes you and facilitates your growth, whether it be a school, a relationship, a job, or truly a home. Go for it! All paths lead home.

Home doesn't have to be where you grew up; family doesn't always mean the people of your birth family. Look at an expanded meaning. Family are people who share the same core values and path. Home can mean a place you have yet to visit or experience, but once there, it feeds your soul in a way that gives you no doubt that you are home.

Alternately, find your safe place. This is where the answers you seek will be found.

44 HOME

Conclusion

My hope for all of you is for a greater awareness of the magnitude and perfection of your soul. Your journey is a sacred one; embrace it and make it memorable! I wish that you would all find that place deep inside that strengthens your ability to be the Heroes of your own story!

Please visit me at
www. michelleamotuzas.com
and share your experiences with your
Shamanic Healing Oracle Deck.